Freedom Matters!

The Connection Between Career, Business, and Freedom

THERE ARE SEVEN TYPES OF LEADERS
NECESSARY FOR FREEDOM TO FLOURISH
Which Type Are You?

New York Times Bestselling Author

OLIVER DEMILLE

OBSTACLES
PRESS

First Edition, February 2015
10 9 8 7 6 5 4 3 2 1

Published by:

 Obstaclés Press
200 Commonwealth Court
Cary, NC 27511

oliverdemille.com

ISBN: 978-0-9909619-7-0

Layout and design by Norm Williams, nwa-inc.com
Cover design by Vernie Lynn DeMille

Printed in the United States of America

If freedom fails,
everything will fail.

CONTENTS

1

FREEDOM AND
LEADERSHIP

*I knew I had made a breakthrough when he came up
during a break and said, "Okay, I finally agree with you."
At my inquiring look, he continued: "I've attended a
number of your speeches before and read all your books,
but I never quite accepted that freedom is a science.
As a medical doctor, I've always thought freedom
seemed like more of an art — not really a science."*

"What changed this time?" I asked.

*"When you explained the seven kinds of leaders
necessary for freedom, it just clicked for me. I realized
that there must be a high level of precision in how the
seven sectors of society are checked and balanced. Before
now, like I said, it seemed kind of abstract. But today
you made it really clear: unless the seven are equal and
effectively balanced with each other, freedom is lost.
That requires precision and rigor, like science."*

"That's right," said the business executive standing next to him. "That piece of knowledge really changes things."

"What do you mean?" I asked her.

"Our careers, our businesses, our families, our education, our health, the world's arts and sciences — everything, in fact — are influenced by freedom. I never saw freedom as art; I thought it was just politics, which I consider less important than art. But today I realized that freedom really is a science and also an art; it has very little to do with politics. It's about creating a specific mathematical-style balance, like a positive balance sheet. Freedom matters — deeply — in our families and every other facet of our lives."

I smiled at their comments. Then my thoughts took a serious turn. "But why does freedom matter so much?" I queried.

They both looked at me in surprise.

Why does freedom matter? People often struggle to answer this question, but ironically, this is only a problem for free people. Those who aren't free, whether they've never lived in a free society or have lost the freedoms they once held, don't wonder how to answer this question.

Not at all. They know how much freedom matters because without it, life is seldom happy. People who aren't free yearn for it, and those who have lost it would do almost anything — *almost anything* — to get it back. When asked why freedom matters, they nearly always answer with tears.

This is why dystopian books like *Utopia, 1984, The Giver*, and *The Hunger Games* can be so powerful for people who are free: reading them offers a taste of why freedom matters.

The Basics

Some things matter because of their physical value in our lives. These include food, shelter, pleasure, pain, sustenance, survival, and all material products—from clothes and shoes to jewelry, cars, houses, electronic devices, and every other material good.

They matter because they help us survive, because we like them, and because they help make our physical lives more successful and enjoyable.

At another level, some things matter because they help make life easier; they help us obtain and protect the physical necessities of life. This level includes economic systems that promote cooperation and progress, institutions that spread prosperity, banks and laws and currencies that help store wealth, governments that protect our life and property from those who would steal or kill, and so on.

Such things make life easier and our efforts to succeed and progress more effective.

The Top Level

Above these, at the top level of things that matter, stand a few vitally important intangibles that are good for their own sake. We all want them—even more than food or shelter—because they naturally determine whether our lives improve, stagnate, or get worse. In fact, they determine all success and progress. They include happiness, spirituality, morality, goodness, love, faith, family, and freedom.

Without this highest level of things that really matter, few people are able to enjoy many of the best physical, emotional, mental, societal, or spiritual benefits in this life. A lack of freedom, for example, results in lives of misery, slavery, servitude, or at the very least, constant struggle merely to survive.

If we don't get the proper physical level of things, we'll die. But if we don't have freedom or goodness or happiness, our lives will often feel worse than death. Living without happiness, goodness, or freedom, we have no hope of ever experiencing anything better.

Freedom Allows the Other Good Things

At this highest level, nothing is more important than freedom and goodness — because freedom and goodness are good for their own sake, like happiness or family, but they also do more than anything else to help us get more of the other things that matter.

Liberty is the ability to make decisions that improve our life. Freedom is a societal environment that allows everyone to make the decisions that improve their lives — that allows all men and women to have liberty.

Without Freedom

Without freedom, our ability to change our lives in any way is blocked. Without freedom, we can't get more physical goods like food or a bigger house or nicer clothes or cars — unless someone else allows us to have them.

Without freedom, we can't get more of the societal benefits like progress or prosperity — unless someone else decides for us.

Without freedom, even our relationships — what we can or can't believe in our religious faith, who we can or can't talk to during the day, what kind of job we can or can't have, who we can or can't marry, how many children we can have and how we raise them, etc. — are determined by other people who rule over us.

At the root, this is what freedom is: the ability to improve our lives by our own choices. When this is taken away, we become dependents — pure and simple. We may be dependent on a king, an aristocracy, or some other ruling caste or elite class, but we are dependent nonetheless.

When the decision to improve our lives — economically, politically, educationally, and/or spiritually — belongs to someone else, we aren't free.

Freedom Has Been Rare in History

Despite the great importance of freedom, throughout history, most people haven't been free. They haven't had the ability to fully choose their own future, or the future of their families and loved ones, for themselves. They've been pawns of other men and women who have made many of the important life choices for them.

The most common way in history to deprive people of their freedom has been simple force. A king, a dictator, or some other kind of tyrant has used power and force to keep people under his or her control. This is a widespread pattern in human history.

The second most common way that people have been dispossessed of their freedoms to choose their own lives has been the use of castes or economic classes — where a small aristocratic or elite group of people have created laws and economic and educational systems that benefitted themselves and kept the rest of the masses firmly under their control.

Freedom Is Rare in Today's World

Both of these systems are alive and well in today's world. Look at the nations of the earth. Most people on the planet are controlled by dictatorships or something very close to this, and nearly all the rest of the people live in societies dominated by a small class of elites.

While it is true that nations ruled by elite classes typically allow more freedom than those run by dictators, both systems reduce the freedom of the people who live under them. People are much freer in the United States, Britain, and Canada than in many of the nations in the Middle East or Asia or Africa, for example, but most of them have significantly less freedom than their grandparents enjoyed. And if current trends continue to centralize power into the elite classes in Europe and North America, our children and grandchildren will have much less freedom than we currently enjoy.

Not on Our Watch!

If this occurs, it will happen on our watch. We are the pivotal generation, the one that will determine whether we value freedom enough to stop its decline. We will pass on to our children and grandchildren in the twenty-first century either a reborn focus on freedom or a rapid loss of freedom to an increasingly powerful, small, dominating, elite ruling class.

This is real. Freedom is in decline.

This is happening—right now, before our very eyes. The question is, what are we going to do about it? If freedom matters, then obviously we need to do whatever is required to stop its decline in our current world.

How Can We Make a Difference, Really?

But what can we do? The answer is surprising in some ways but clear and obvious in others. It's one of those thoughts that occurs to few people, but when we hear it, we immediately realize that it is the obvious answer.

The future of freedom depends on leadership.

Leadership is another of the highest level of things that matter, and it stands at a level just slightly above the rest—because if the right leadership occurs, freedom and goodness and the other great things will happen. If leadership doesn't take place, they won't.

Most people instinctively understand this, which is why so many people hope that some great political leader will win an election and fix their nation. This hope is seldom realized, but people tend to cling to it regardless. They know that the right kind of leadership can do amazing things, so they keep waiting and hoping for it to come.

A Grave Misunderstanding about Politics

The problem is that most of us have misunderstood exactly what kinds of leaders are needed. People tend to think that the solution will come from a great political leader, but this is only part of the equation—a relatively minor part, actually.

Through history, there have been a few times when the right kind of political leader—Abraham, Moses, Solon, Marcus Aurelius, Josiah, Joan of Arc, George Washington, Abraham Lincoln, Winston Churchill, and so on—has come along and done great things to put society on the right path.

But in all these cases, the great political leader was able to do his or her work because of something that already existed in the society. Political leadership is important, but it is only one of seven kinds of vital leadership.

No society succeeds unless all seven kinds of leaders are doing their jobs well. And political leaders are the weakest of the seven; in fact, freedom and goodness only spread in a society when the other six kinds of leadership are flourishing. And unless the other six kinds of leaders are truly fulfilling their purpose, political leaders can't get the traction needed to make real or lasting changes.

Seven Kinds of Leaders, Not Just One Political Leader

This is where our society finds itself today. We want political leaders to fix things, but they can't do it alone. They never will, until the other six kinds of leaders do a better job. Freedom only flourishes when these six kinds of leaders excel, and today, all six are struggling.

History is clear on this point: Political leaders only succeed when the other six kinds of leaders really deliver. The other six kinds of leadership must come first.

If and when we see the rise of the right kind of influence in our society from these six kinds of leaders, we'll see political leaders do great things. Until then, we won't. Write it in stone. This is true.

You Are the Problem

The problem isn't in Washington, Ottawa, Tokyo, London, Paris, or any capital city. It is found in our homes and our neighborhoods, our schools and our businesses. The problem can be seen in our mirrors. Look yourself in the eyes, and ask if you are excelling at one of these six kinds of leadership in your life.

If not, the problem is simple. The problem is you. Me. All of us.

The good news is that this problem is relatively easy to solve. Find out which of the six kinds of leadership (seven, really, including political leadership) is your life purpose. Once you know this, excel at your life mission. This creates the kind of leadership we need.

This will fix America. *Only* this will fix America or Canada, Mexico, Brazil, Germany, Kenya, Australia, China, or whatever nation you live in. The answers aren't found in capital cities, from Washington to Beijing to Ottawa. The political leaders will only really be able to lead when the other six kinds of leaders are truly doing their part.

- Which kind of leader are you?
- How can you lead at a much better, higher level?

The future of freedom depends on the answers to these two questions. Freedom and goodness matter. The future of millions in your nation, and billions in the world, depends on the quality of your leadership.

Six Kinds of Leaders Must Take a Stand

When the six kinds of leaders truly excel, nations improve and thrive. When the six kinds of leaders really shine, great political leaders naturally arise and fix big problems.

But when the six kinds of leaders play it small, focus on narrow things, don't live up to their potential, or settle for anything less than truly great leadership, politicians bluster and bumble, and politics worsen. Freedom and goodness always decline in such an environment. Corruption and immorality win the battle — day after day, year after year.

So much depends on leadership. Leadership matters. When leadership does its part, in all seven ways, freedom and goodness spread, become popular, and overcome all challenges.

This is our world today, and you are at the center of the future. If you, and others like you in the seven arenas of leadership, rise to your leadership potential, the future of freedom, goodness, prosperity, and happiness is bright. If not, we will continue to decline.

The future is up to you. First, clearly determine which of the seven kinds of leadership you should excel in. Second, do it. Give your heart and soul to it. Make it your life focus and life purpose.

This is the path, the only path, to a future of freedom and greatness.

Let's find out more about the seven kinds of leadership.

"The only freedom which deserves the name
is that of pursuing our own good in our own way,
so long as we do not attempt to deprive others of theirs
or impede their efforts to obtain it."
— JOHN STUART MILL

2

THE SEVEN LEADERS

When the pilot announced the descent of our flight, the man turned to me and asked, "Which of the seven kinds of leaders are you? You're a teacher and a speaker, but it seems to me that your real mission is freedom, not education. They're pretty closely related, I guess. But which of the seven sectors is your main focus?"

I cocked my head to one side and considered. "Well...I think everyone should be a good family leader. If I had to pick just one, family would be my focus. In fact, if everyone did this well, most of our national problems would be quickly solved."

He nodded. "I agree. But I sense you feel a deep mission in one of the other sectors as well, right?"

In our three-hour conversation during the flight, I had learned that this man, despite his dress in beach clothes and his favorite hobby of scuba diving, had a quick and deep mind. As an engineer, he was accustomed to thinking about things far beyond surface answers.

"I guess I'm a media or artistic leader, if I have to choose just one," I told him. "My books, articles, and speeches emphasize the need for freedom and how only people who understand the principles of freedom — truly and deeply — can really be the leaders we need. No nation that is run by any one group of elites or politicians remains free.

"The problem," I continued, "is that too many media leaders, artists, and even religious, academic, and community leaders tend to see government officials as more important to freedom than business leaders. And I think this view is downright wrong. So I hesitate to call myself a media leader, even though my main focus is writing articles and books and creating audios that spread the truth about freedom."

He smiled and then replied, "The carpenter thinks every problem can be fixed with a hammer, but you are saying that we need many, many tools to really maintain a free society. Everybody should participate because the businessman has just as much, maybe more, to offer than the politician."

I smiled. "Yes, and just like I think most people should be family leaders, I also think most of us should be business leaders as well. Whatever other role we serve, we should spread opportunity, prosperity, and ownership. Entrepreneurship, in all fields, creates a nation of leaders."

Freedom exists, and lasts, to the exact extent that the seven kinds of leaders are all doing their main role in society. When any of them fall short, freedom declines. When any of them rise above and control the others, freedom declines. Freedom could easily be defined as the state of balance between all seven kinds of leadership.

The seven kinds of leaders are:

- Family Leaders
- Religious/Ethical Leaders
- Business Leaders
- Education Leaders
- Media/Artistic Leaders
- Community Leaders
- Government Leaders

Again, freedom thrives when all seven are strong because they naturally check and balance each other, keeping any one type of leader from dominating the others. When one or two of these sectors rule or control the others, freedom weakens and is eventually lost.

To make this even simpler, there are two main types of leaders in a free society, specifically *officials* and *entrepreneurs*. Officials lead in the government sector, and entrepreneurs are the leaders of all the other six sectors. While some people assume that entrepreneurship is mainly about the business sector, this is too narrow a definition. To succeed as a leader in any of the six private sectors, a person needs the skills of entrepreneurship.

This is what free enterprise is all about: voluntarily taking the risk to attempt something that is needed. Sometimes this is in business, but it is also needed in the other sectors as well. Officials lead the government sector, and entrepreneurs are those who "enterprise" what is needed in all six private sectors.

Balance #1

This is the delicate balance of freedom. If any of the seven kinds of leaders fall short or become much stronger than the others, freedom is in danger.

Such imbalances happen more often than not. In fact, freedom has been extremely rare in human history for this very reason. For example, consider what happens if government dominates the other six kinds of leadership. The result is dictatorship or what the American founders called tyranny. This actually has been the norm in world history, unfortunately.

When governments control religion, most freedom is lost. The same is true when governments control the press or education. Freedom is lost when governments control basic family choices or business enterprise.

In short, when government leaders control any (or all) of the other six, through lots of regulation or any other kind of government power, freedom quickly deteriorates. Modern conservatives are very concerned about such a system, and this is why they generally mistrust big government.

Balance #2

But government control of the other six sectors is not the only factor that destroys freedom. Freedom declines and is eventually extinguished when *any* one of the seven sectors dominates any of the other six.

When business motives dominate churches, for example, morality becomes whatever is most popular, most marketable, and easiest to sell. Profit shouldn't rule religion. When businesses dominate government, the society becomes an aristocracy — where the wealthy run everything and the lower and middle classes are kept forever in their inferior station.

When businesses run education, schools can begin to care less about knowledge and learning and focus instead on the credentials and status that support the goals and agendas of an elite upper class. And so on.

Just as conservatives are very concerned about the problems caused by big government, liberals and progressives have historically been very uneasy about the damage done in societies by big business. When the business sector rules above the other six sectors, freedom is lost to big, aristocratic elitism and a few wealthy and powerful ruling families.

No wonder both conservatives and liberals are so adamant about their beliefs. Their dedication to protecting society from the dangers of big government and big business, respectively, are very important. Sadly, many people often get so caught up in this battle between the two sides that they lose sight of the real war: the loss of freedom to a ruling upper class of *any* kind.

Balance #3

Freedom deteriorates whenever there is an imbalance between the seven sectors. For example, when religious leaders dominate the other six sectors of society, they often turn to excesses, such as the Crusades or the Inquisition. This is very damaging to people and societies because when it occurs, one church nearly always gains all the political power — and usually ends religious freedom with force by attacking other churches. History shows that this is always very harmful to society.

Liberals have historically been very concerned about this danger, and in American history, conservatives have also considered this a major potential threat to the happiness of the people. For the American founders, the solution was to protect the right of people to believe as they choose—so long as they do no harm to others—and to ensure that no religious test is required for political leaders.

The founders wanted people to have the freedom to worship and believe without government interference and also to create a model where no one church could rule everyone else (including other religions) by controlling the government. They had seen or read about this happening repeatedly in European history, and they knew it was a real danger.

Such an imbalance stems from two dangers, in fact: 1) government controlling religion or 2) one church controlling government and using its power to shut down religious freedom. The framers set up America to be religiously free and avoid both of these problems.

Balance #4

But there are still more ways to reduce a nation's freedoms. Again, all that is necessary is for one sector to rule one or more of the other six. This is clearly bad when government rules the others (tyranny, dictatorship), when big business forcefully rules the rest (aristocracy, elitism), or when a single church has the government power to dominate the other six sectors (inquisition).

But what could possibly be wrong with families or communities dominating the other six sectors? How could this do any harm?

Actually, this has produced some of the worst systems in history. When families dominate the other six kinds of leadership (business, government, religion, education, etc.), the result is a mafia system — where a few families rise to the height of power and usually clash until one or two of these family organizations rule the whole society with violence, corruption, and an iron fist.

As for communities dominating the other six kinds of leadership, this is one of the nastiest societal systems — usually resulting in communism, gulags, prison camps, torture, and secret police. In such systems, a few leaders claim the good of the community as a reason to force, hurt, control, and dominate almost everyone in the nation.

This kind of communal/communistic approach created mass graves and mass misery in modern Russia, China, Eastern Europe, and many other places around the world. Community leadership plays a vital role in society, but when it dominates families, religions, businesses, the media, the arts, education, and governments, it becomes a major enemy of freedom.

Balance #5

Actually, throughout history, even bigger problems have come when *two* of the seven sectors have joined together to dominate the other five. This kind of imbalance includes:

- business and government dominating the nation (fascism; e.g., Germany and Italy in the 1930s–1940s)
- government and one church dominating the nation (inquisition; e.g., Southern Europe during the Dark Ages)

- government and community ruling the rest of society, with government as the lead (communism; e.g., twentieth-century Russia, China, and Cuba)
- community and government dictating to the other sectors of a nation, with communal forces as the lead (socialism; e.g., much of nineteenth- and twentieth-century Western Europe)
- families and government controlling everyone else (mafia; e.g., medieval Italy)
- education and government directing the nation (rule by experts/credentialist social democracy; e.g., post–World War I and II Germany)
- any other arrangement where all seven kinds of leadership aren't equal or where one or two of the seven kinds of leadership dominate the rest by taking over the force-based role of government

Check #1

In short, freedom exists when two conditions thrive:

1. a balance of all seven kinds of leadership in society, with none ruling the others

2. strong leadership in all seven sectors that checks abuses by any other sector

If we want to live in a free society and pass a legacy of freedom on to our children and grandchildren, it is essential to create and perpetuate these two conditions.

Today we are weak in both, especially the first. For decades, the United States has witnessed a decreasing balance between the seven sectors of leadership, as central government and big business have become more and more dominant over the other five and, at the same time, government has increasingly dominated business.

If this seems too strongly stated, simply consider two quick questions. First, compared to 1921, 1945, or 1970, for example, how many more government regulations do we have today that try to control families, schools, farming, hospitals, businesses, media outlets, accountants, engineers, construction, food production, transportation, churches, etc.?

The truth is that in some of these sectors, we have well over a hundred times more regulations, laws, rules, agency policies, mandates, licensing, fines, taxation, and other government requirements than we did in 1921. In fact, try to name a sector that has less government oversight than it did in 1921.

It simply doesn't exist. The sad reality is that in some cases, the amount of regulation has drastically increased. And every increase brings a reduction of freedom, unless families or other kinds of leaders have the same amount of increased control over government. But they don't. Most typical family, business, church, school, or journalistic institutions have almost the same amount of control over government, or less, as they did in 1921.

But the government has increased its control by hundreds during this same era. This growing imbalance is the decline of freedom, pure and simple. And it is increasing today at a higher rate than ever before in American history.

Check #2

Second, at the same time, big business is also widening the gap of power over the other sectors of society (everything except government and business). For example, just consider how many churches operated like for-profit businesses in 1935 versus how many run like corporations today.

Indeed, in 1935, very few churches in the United States saw themselves as business entities. Nearly all religious leaders of that era would have been highly offended to hear their churches called businesses. But today, many would be insulted if you called them anything but professional, modernized organizations that apply the best business practices.

The same is true of most schools in 1935 and of most media organizations in the same year. They saw themselves as bastions of knowledge and truth, as teachers and journalists standing against crass materialism and for the highest ideals. Today nearly all schools and media institutions are simply big business; many are even owned by corporations and run as for-profit companies. Even most of those holding nonprofit status still operate as big businesses—though often not nearly as well.

In fact, many states require colleges and universities to drop majors and degrees with no proven commercial purpose that prepares students for money-making careers and jobs. This is a total reversal of what higher education stood for in early America. So much for the ideals of the American academy, the lofty idea that education is about knowledge and truth and a voice against mere money for money's sake.

When churches, schools, and journalists are run by corporations and the focus is profit, business and government dominate these sectors, and freedom is naturally weakened.

Check #3

This is not to say that there is anything wrong with business, prosperity, or profit. Quite the opposite is true. Business has a vital—*absolutely vital*—role to play in freedom, happiness, and progress in society. But when government exerts extensive controls on the business sector, freedom and prosperity suffer. Likewise, when churches, schools, and journalistic endeavors are simply business ventures, none of them stand solely for truth and goodness.

We need a strong, vibrant sector of society that stands for prosperity, wealth, and abundance. This is the vitally important business leadership role in any free nation. Without thriving entrepreneurialism in business and all six private sectors, freedom always declines. Sadly, when the government overregulates, a natural result is to turn media and educational voices against free enterprise—instead of against depraved or corrupt materialism.

This is ironic because in such situations, good, family-blessing businesses and entrepreneurial ventures are often ridiculed at the same time that profitable pursuits like gambling, recreational intoxicants, and even prostitution are encouraged in some circles.

In addition to flourishing free enterprise, we also need a sector of society that stands strongly for morality and truth, even though this means choosing the right when the values of profit and righteousness sometimes come into conflict. This is the role of churches and religious leadership.

We also need a sector that stands as a champion of knowledge—not just commercially profitable knowledge but *all* knowledge and learning. This is the purpose of education leadership.

We need a sector that defends wisdom in society, checking and balancing the excesses of government and any other sector that tries to gain too much control over the people. Such a sector focuses on keeping all seven sectors in balance with each other. This is the noble place of media and the arts—or at least it should be.

Take any of these away, and freedom is reduced. Its demise comes slowly or rapidly, depending on how weak any of these sectors and their leaders become.

Check #4

Again, freedom blossoms when all seven sectors, and their leaders, are strong but also equal. They are meant to check each other, and none are meant to work for each other or take over the roles of any other sector.

When government takes over the media, as in the old Soviet Union, freedom is lost. When government takes over education, as in much of the current world (just look at Germany), freedom is greatly weakened. When government becomes the top promoter of morality (or whatever it defines as such), taking over for religious leaders while simultaneously attacking them, freedom declines.

This list goes on and on. When schools become businesses, they work for profit—not knowledge. When media is highly regulated, it works for government—not wisdom or checks on big government. When communities take over the raising of children from parents, they become socialists—not promoters of voluntary service, charitable works, and neighborhood synergy and cooperation. When...

Well, you get the point. In all of these instances, freedom is under attack. It is attacked whenever leaders of one sector take over the roles of another sector. It is attacked whenever leaders of one sector allow their sector to be overtaken by another. When there is decline—as we are experiencing right now—leadership is weak.

Check #5

Freedom is also attacked whenever the leaders of a sector fail to stand firmly and strongly against any loss of power to the other sectors. It is under attack whenever the leaders of a sector fail to truly excel in their main role.

Check and Balance #6

Finally, there is one more vital principle that we must all understand if we are going to maintain freedom in any society or nation. This law of freedom is unbending and must always be followed. In fact, it is both a check and a balance that protects freedom.

It is this: While leadership in any of the six private sectors can be a person's life mission and purpose, government leaders must be found among the leaders of the other six sectors.

In other words, government leadership should not be a primary life mission. It is a secondary mission, something that brings together leaders from the other six sectors to help with government decisions for a time. When a class of politicians or bureaucrats, or both, become a full-time caste of government leaders, freedom is in grave danger.

In all of history, freedom has only lasted when there was no enduring, full-time, lifetime sector of government leaders. To repeat, freedom only lasts when a nation's government is made up of leaders who have built a lifetime of service and work in a combination of the other six sectors.

This is absolutely essential.

The Science of Freedom

In summary, while liberty is the ability to make choices that improve your life and the lives of those you care about, freedom is a system where all men and women enjoy this same set of choices — as long as they don't choose to hurt others in the process.

Freedom exists in history only when all seven sectors of society have strong leaders and when these sectors are equal to each other, none are dominated by another, and all share a balanced part in leading the society.

This is freedom. Anything else always falls short.

This is, in fact, the science of freedom, the mathematical balance of seven types of leaders. If any one type dominates the others or if any one type becomes too weak, freedom declines.

This high ideal has seldom been achieved in history, and it has never lasted for long. But we have come close more than once. Each time, the closer we have gotten to a true balance of leadership between all seven sectors, the more genuine freedom has been enjoyed by more people.

If we want to reverse our current decline and save freedom in our time, we need to get closer to this vital balance of leadership. Specifically, we need strong leaders in each of the six private sectors, and those leaders from each of the six working with each other in the seventh sector (government), to more fully understand and fulfill their roles.

The future of freedom depends on leadership. *Your* leadership, to be precise. It depends on your leadership focused on a specific role in society. On your career and your business. The link between your career, business, and freedom is unavoidable.

Whatever your career or business, it fits into one of the six sectors of free society. Your leadership in your career is essential for freedom — but only if you lead in the right way.

"Liberty means responsibility.
That is why most men dread it."
—GEORGE BERNARD SHAW

3

FREEDOM AND FREE ENTERPRISE

"Seriously," she asked. "What do you mean by the word freedom? It isn't totally clear to me. You use it a lot, but you seem to mean something by it that I just don't quite grasp. Can you please define it, slowly and thoroughly?"

I looked at her in surprise. "Doesn't everyone know the answer to your question?" I asked.

I could tell by the faces in the room that many of the people didn't know.

"Maybe everyone but me knows," she replied, "but I'm unclear. Please just take a minute and help me understand."

I nodded and then asked the group: "Are liberty and freedom the same thing?"

A few nods. Mostly blank stares.

> *"Okay," I looked at her with respect. "I think*
> *you've hit on something very important. Let's take*
> *a moment and define some fundamental terms."*

To give more depth to the way we define *freedom* throughout this book and in our society, we first need to define *liberty*. After all, the Declaration of Independence boldly affirms that among our inalienable rights are "life, liberty, and the pursuit of happiness."

Important Definitions

Liberty and freedom are similar, but they are slightly different, and understanding them both is essential in a society that is losing its freedoms. I think the most accurate definition of *liberty* is "the right to do whatever a person wants as long as it doesn't violate the inalienable rights of anyone else."

Of course, in order to exercise liberty, people need to know what inalienable rights are; otherwise, they won't know whether or not they are violating them. Thus, knowledge and wisdom are required to maintain one's liberty because those who violate somebody else's inalienable rights naturally forfeit their own liberty.

The extent of this forfeiture is equivalent to the depth of the violation. When this is applied well, it is called *justice*.

License, as opposed to liberty, is defined as "the power to do whatever a person wants or is able to do." Note that this has often been used in history as an excuse to plunder, force, or otherwise violate the rights of others. Thus, license and tyranny are nearly always connected: the tyrant is tyrannical precisely because he or she takes license as he or she wills, and any person who keeps pursuing license eventually exerts tyranny of some kind.

Sometimes people pick one of the inalienable rights and use it to define *liberty* as, for example, "the right to do whatever a person wants as long as it doesn't violate the property of another" or "...the life of another," etc. The problem with this type of definition is that though it is often narrowly accurate, it is also too limited. The violation of *any* inalienable right takes away one's liberty.

Now that we have a definition of *liberty*, we can also define and compare the meaning of *freedom*:

Liberty: the right to do whatever a person wants as long as it doesn't violate the inalienable rights of anyone else.

Freedom: a societal arrangement that guarantees the right of each person to do whatever he or she wants as long as it doesn't violate the inalienable rights of anyone else.

Freedom Needed

Liberty comes from the Latin root *liber* through the French *liberté*, meaning "free will, freedom to do as one chooses... absence of restraint."[1] In contrast, the word *freedom* is rooted in the Old English *freodom,* which meant "state of free will; charter, emancipation, deliverance."[2] Thus, liberty can exist with or without government, but freedom is a widespread societal system that requires some authority to maintain it.

In most eras of history, the goal has been liberty, but liberty is almost never maintained without freedom. In other words, it is possible to have liberty without freedom, but in such cases, it seldom lasts long and is usually enjoyed by only a limited few (the upper class).

When freedom is present, however, liberty exists for all who don't violate the inalienable rights of others.

Today's Mission

This journey through history has a vitally important current application. A lot of people want liberty; in fact, nearly everyone desires liberty. But the only duty of liberty is to personally honor the inalienable rights of everyone else, and as a result, liberty without freedom is fleeting.

In contrast, freedom requires many more duties, and therefore, it musters much more from its people. It only succeeds when the large majority of people in a society voluntarily fulfill many duties that keep the whole civilization free.

Specifically, freedom only thrives when all seven kinds of leaders discussed earlier in this book do their part — and when none of them take over the roles of the others. This is likely what Gandhi meant when he reportedly taught the idea that we should "be the change [we] wish to see in the world."

To repeat: Those who stand for freedom must honor the inalienable rights of all, and they must also take responsibility for standing up and helping ensure that society succeeds. No truly free government directs this free and voluntary behavior, but without it, freedom decreases.

The Most Important Key to Freedom

For example, one of the duties of those who support freedom is *free enterprise* — in all six private types of leadership. Free enterprise involves voluntarily (freely) taking actions (enterprises) that improve the society and make it better.

No government should penalize a person who does not do this, who doesn't serve and lead in any of the six areas of leadership, because such penalties would reduce freedom. But overall freedom will decrease if a person has the potential to undertake great enterprises that improve the world but doesn't do so.

This is the unbreakable connection between career, business, and freedom. *If people don't voluntarily use their business and career life to do good things that protect and spread freedom, nothing the government does to protect freedom will ultimately work.*

Freedom depends on most working adults choosing actions that promote long-term societal success. If the adults in a society don't use their work to benefit freedom—if they instead just focus on themselves—the whole nation suffers, and freedom goes into decline.

Sadly, most people don't realize this. Freedom is very demanding. If people don't voluntarily do good things—and great things—in all six private sectors of leadership (family, church, community, education, media/arts, and business), freedom declines. If they don't exert their will and take risks to improve the world through their families, volunteer service, business, and careers, freedom stagnates and decreases.

Another way that people voluntarily increase freedom is by choosing morality. In societies where a lot of the people don't choose a moral life, liberty may be maintained by a few people, but the freedom of all people declines. When more people choose the path of virtuous living, freedom grows.

The same is true of charity and service. When more people choose these, freedom increases. There are a number of other ways people can voluntarily take actions that have a direct and positive impact on freedom. In the freest societies, a lot of the people choose to engage in many such voluntary behaviors that protect and spread freedom.

A Pledge

This all applies to learning as well. If citizens choose not to study the writings of freedom, they'll see their own freedoms decline. Nobody makes them do such study—to do so would be to reduce freedom directly—but without it, freedom doesn't flourish. It can't.

When Americans pledge allegiance to the flag, for example, we do so to promote "liberty and justice for all." This is the role of government: liberty and justice or, in other words, the protection of inalienable rights and the providing of recompense if such rights are violated.

But while in free nations government is limited to this role, the *people* in a free society must do much more. If they all do their best, fully living up to their potential, leading in the six private sectors of society, freedom greatly increases.

In other words, the real question isn't "What is freedom?" but rather "What is *your role* in freedom?"

The answer is different for each person, but the key is that your focus (and my focus and each individual's focus) should be simply "Am I living up to my full potential, my great life mission and purpose in this world, and becoming an excellent leader in one or more of the six sectors that promote freedom?"

If your answer to this question is "Yes," you are a leader of freedom, and your efforts and projects will help increase freedom for everyone.

If not, now is the time to get started. You stand at the crossroads of freedom's future, and your actions matter. Freedom flourishes only when the regular citizens make voluntary choices that increase education, charity, morality, leadership, service, philanthropy, and prosperity—and use their careers and businesses to do so. When a people stops doing this, for whatever reason, freedom declines.

If you are an adult, your responsibility to freedom is clear. Become a leader in one of the six private areas of freedom leadership. Then become a better leader in your chosen area.

It's really that simple. But when most adults don't do this in a society, decline naturally occurs.

If you are not doing this, you are helping the decline of freedom and our society, whether or not you consciously make this choice. This is very real. Next time you are on the street or in a place with a lot of people, look around. Some of the people are helping freedom, and others are hurting it.

How can you tell the difference? Which of the people are voluntarily using their careers, business, work, and free time to spread one or more of the six private areas of freedom leadership (family, education, morality, service, business, and truth)? Those who are giving their time and lives to promote these sectors are standing up for freedom. The others are not.

"[T]o a benevolent human mind, there can be no spectacle presented by any nation, more pleasing, more noble, majestic, or august, than an assembly...of a Government...in which the Executive authority, as well as that of all the branches of the Legislature, are exercised by citizens selected at regular periods by their neighbors to make and execute laws for the general good."
—JOHN ADAMS

4

THE VITAL ROLE OF BUSINESS LEADERS

*He shook his head and said, "I just
don't quite understand you."*

"Why not?" I asked in surprise.

*"Well, we agree on so many things. In the realm of freedom,
we agree on almost everything. But it's strange to me that
you were a teacher for so many years, and now a writer.
I'm just not used to people in academia or the media who
think business has an important role in freedom."*

*"Are you kidding?" I protested. "Entrepreneurship
is arguably the most important role in free society.
Of course, family leadership, religious leaders — these
are just as vital. But ultimately, nothing is more
important than the initiative, innovation, frugality,
and ingenuity that successful entrepreneurs bring to
a nation. Without these, freedom always fails."*

*He smiled at my outburst and said, "I agree. I'm just
surprised to hear you say it. I'm a business leader, after
all. I'm just excited to hear that you feel the same."*

*"Without great business leaders," I continued,
"freedom never lasts. Never. The main role of business
leaders is enterprise — doing things voluntarily that
lead a society to whole new levels of success and
taking the risks to make this happen. Without this,
there simply is no progress and no freedom."*

Each of the seven sectors in society has a vital role. The role
of business is enterprise. This means taking good risks. Unless
this is done well, no society experiences real progress. But when
it is done well, consistently over time, the amount of progress
is often huge.

No other sector can take such risks as well or effectively
as business entrepreneurs. This is why the central values of
entrepreneurship are, among others, initiative, innovation,
tenacity, and success. Innovation is necessary for progress, and
there is no innovation without risk. In fact, if everyone agrees
with you, as entrepreneur Orrin Woodward put it, you're not
really innovating.

The Price of Risk

But there is an even deeper reason that entrepreneurial
business leadership is so essential. Think of it this way: if family
leaders took most of the innovative risks in society to try out
new things and new ways of doing things, what would happen
if many of them failed? The truth is, with risk, even wise risk,
comes a higher rate of failure than when no risk is involved.

If many families took massive risks, a lot of children would bear the brunt of society's struggles for progress. A long time ago, people decided that children shouldn't carry this burden. Childhood, first as tradition and later as law, was given a special protection, a time to learn and grow with less risk than the other sectors of society.

Likewise, what if churches were the constant innovators? When they failed at higher-than-average rates—the necessary result of taking lots of risk—their role of teaching the truth would be always in peril. They would lose credibility and the strength of standing on principle even when the other sectors of society were willing to take risks.

Governments that constantly risked everything would fail at a higher-than-average rate, and the result would be massive loss of life, liberty, and the pursuit of happiness. This isn't a good role for government because its role to protect inalienable rights should brook as little risk as possible.

In short, the six nonbusiness sectors have roles that are too important to risk over money. But without risk to increase prosperity, very little progress will occur.

This is one way in which the business sector greatly benefits society. Business entrepreneurs certainly take risks to create more wealth, but their choices usually don't directly risk the truth, morality, or the inalienable rights of the nation's people.

They risk money, time, and effort. And they risk only their own money or that of other business entrepreneurs who voluntarily choose to invest in their project. On the one hand, this tends to reduce risk to those projects that can justify funding by someone. On the other hand, when a business entrepreneur's project fails, the entrepreneur and his or her investors lose their money without bringing down the whole nation, government, church, or community.

If there are no business entrepreneurs in your nation, there is no consistent increase of wealth or prosperity. There is very little progress, if any at all. If there are a lot of business entrepreneurs in your society, however, there is a lot of wealth and prosperity. If you are a business entrepreneur, you can attain wealth and help many others do the same.

This is, indeed, a fabulous role in society. Business leaders are vitally important to freedom. Along with courageous entrepreneurs in the other private sectors of society, they are the leaders of enterprise.

Enterprise means starting something new, innovating, or using ingenuity to do something in a better way. The truth is that the level of success and happiness in any society is a direct result of enterprise. The more and better the enterprises, the more success, prosperity, and happiness there is to go around. This blesses families, schools, churches, and communities, but it isn't their main focus.

When individuals and leaders in all sectors of society have the freedom to pursue the enterprises they deem important or desirable, as long as they don't infringe upon the inalienable rights of anyone else, this is called free enterprise.

Government's role is to protect this freedom and leave the enterprising to the other six sectors of society. This is the *only* good and proper role for government. Anything else hurts freedom.

The level of any society's success and progress is directly determined by the level of free enterprise protected by the government and what individuals and groups do with their enterprises. Since nearly all enterprises, in all seven sectors, require money and resources to achieve the highest levels of success, the business sector is essential. In fact, as philosopher, author, and diplomat Michael Novak put it, business is a very important "calling" in life.

If this is your calling, you are a vital warrior for freedom. You probably don't see yourself this way, since your focus is on turning work and investment into increased value to society. But those who do this successfully are essential to the protection and spreading of freedom.

Business Knowledge 101

This brings us to certain basic knowledge every citizen must know. Most business and other leaders in the seven sectors don't fully understand the following material, and this hurts their ability to turn their career and life into real leadership for freedom.

As I have written elsewhere: "There are two major types of economies: *market* economies and *command* economies. The first is based on freedom, the second on force. Within these two branches there are a number of subtypes, including various kinds of command economies such as socialism, communism, fascism, collectivism, and different applications of economic authoritarianism and totalitarianism.

"The divisions of market-style economies are sometimes more confusing to people from free societies, because most of us have been trained to evaluate political and economic issues in binary mode where we narrow any debate down to only two sides—such as liberal vs. conservative, socialist vs. capitalist, democratic vs. totalitarian, good or evil, Allies or Axis, believers and atheists, idealists and realists, free or not free, and so on.

"That said, we live in an era where the various types of market economics are now in conflict. During the Cold War the world was divided between two great camps, with market economies of all types firmly allied against the command economies, the NATO nations of the West versus the Soviet Bloc and world communism. But after the Cold War and especially in the post-9/11 world, this has dramatically changed. There are forces supporting each of the various types of market economies, and often these are pitted against each other in ways unthinkable before the fall of the Berlin Wall in 1989.

"Differentiating between these subtypes is important for anyone who wants to accurately understand what is happening in today's world."[3] Real leaders especially must understand the differences. "When people use the term 'capitalism,' they may be referring to any of the following five types of market economies. But the truth is that each of these models has drastically different goals and processes:

- **Mercantilism:** A system where the law allows market forces but gives preference and special benefits to the sector of the economy owned (or directly controlled) by the government. This system was historically used by the British Empire.

- **Corporatism:** A system where the law encourages market forces and also gives preference and special benefits to the sector of the economy owned by big corporations within the nation, sometimes referred to as 'Big Business,' 'The Military-Industrial Complex,' or simply 'The Establishment.'

- **Keynesianism:** A system where the law allows market forces but gives preference and special benefits to companies and institutions that are so big that they tend to care more about their public image for societal responsibility and promoting social justice than about profit(s), market share or stock value.

- **Capitalism:** A system where the law encourages market forces and also gives preference and special benefits to the sector of the economy owned by big capital — including big corporations like in Corporatism, but also wealthy foreign and multinational corporations, and highly influential non-corporate institutions such as rich foundations, moneyed trusts, political parties, well-funded lobbies and special interest groups, affluent non-profit entities, wealthy families, moneyed foreign investors, and others with large amounts of capital. Under this system, the rich rule society, and they naturally influence government to maintain policies that benefit the rich more than others.

- **Free Enterprise:** A system where the law encourages market forces and gives no special preferences; it protects equal rights for all individuals and entities and leaves initiative and enterprise to private individuals, groups, businesses and organizations that are all treated equally and with minimal legislation by the legal code....

"All five of these subtypes are market-based, and sometimes called 'free market' or simply 'market economy' systems.... For the last three generations, these five types of market economics have frequently been lumped together under the label of 'capitalism.' While this is technically inaccurate — because capitalism is a subtype rather than the whole of market economics — this is the way the word 'capitalism' has been used by most people.

"Under this popular definition, capitalism is synonymous with 'market economics' and is a label for the entire free-market model. But even when people use this broader definition, it is important to distinguish which of the five types is being discussed—because the future of freedom under capitalism, corporatism or mercantilism will be a very different reality than it would be under true free enterprise.

"So, to summarize, we have five definitions of 'capitalism' in the current usage, and another definition which uses 'capitalism' to refer to all the five types together. Naturally, these definitions are frequently confused in our contemporary language. Note that even the broader definition of 'capitalism' includes every market approach from corporatism and Keynesianism to mercantilism and the more narrow meaning of capitalism.

"In all of this, free enterprise is often forgotten. Even worse, in the realm of modern politics all five of these systems are frequently lumped together and referred to as 'democracy' or simply 'freedom.' While this is a partially accurate definition, it confuses the fact that these five kinds of democracies behave very differently and offer different results to society."[4] And leaders of all seven sectors of society are at the center of these differences.

"Again, this is confusing to most people, but understanding the details and nuances of how these words are used is extremely important to maintain freedom. The American founders dealt with several similar language challenges, such as when Madison felt the need to write *Federalist Papers* 10 and 14 explaining the important differences between democracies and republics.

"He also used papers 18, 19 and 20 to clarify the differences between federations and confederations, as well as national versus federal governments. Without such clarity, the

Constitution would have been confusing to many Americans who were deciding whether or not to ratify it.

"The fact that today most Americans don't understand these differences illustrates how far we have devolved from the level of education exemplified by the founding generation. There are numerous similar examples, and part of being a free people is taking the time to understand the nuances of economic and political freedom and the language of liberty.

"No nation in history has maintained freedom at a level deeper than that understood by the regular citizens in the society. And note that few things are more essential for free people than clearly understanding what type of economic system they want."[5]

Leaders, more than anyone else, need to truly understand these differences. They are the leaders of free enterprise, and they must understand what it really is, how it really works, and whether or not any government policy is for or against it. They must know these things so well that they quickly realize how any government proposal will help or hurt free enterprise and any or all of the six private sectors. And they must teach this to the rest of us.

This is a vital role of all leaders in a free nation.

Three Observations
"Based on the definitions above, consider the following three observations:

- First, all five types of market economies are better (meaning they have more freedom, opportunity and prosperity for more people) than all types of command economies.

Even the market approaches with the least freedom (Keynesianism and mercantilism) are significantly better than the command systems with the most freedom (collectivism and socialism).

- Second, when comparing the five subtypes of market economies, free enterprise is significantly better (with more freedom, opportunity and prosperity for more people) than mercantilism, corporatism, capitalism, and/ or Keynesianism.

- Third, the United States, Canada, Britain, France, Japan and other leading free nations of the world today have far too much mercantilism, corporatism, capitalism, and Keynesianism—and not enough free enterprise.

"This is surprising to most citizens in America and the free world. For example, many in the United States argue that we are a 'capitalist' nation or vote for the 'capitalist' candidate and conclude that all is well, when in fact free enterprise is under attack from socialism but also just as strongly from mercantilists, corporatists, Keynesians and capitalists. Voters and citizens must know what to look for when a policy or candidate claims to promote 'capitalism.'

Real-Life Differences

"Some might argue that most of this is mere theory, and that the United States today is a free enterprise society rather than a capitalist system as outlined here. Such an assumption is incorrect. The U.S. commercial code has numerous laws that are written specifically to treat people differently based on their wealth—and extending special benefits to those with more capital.

"For example, it is illegal for those with less than a certain amount of wealth to be offered many of the best investment opportunities. Only those with a high net worth (the amount is set by law) are able to invest in such offerings. This is capitalism, not free enterprise. Under free enterprise, the law would be the same for all people.

"Also, in many cities employees of the wealthy are allowed special legal benefits—such as carrying firearms (personally or through bodyguards), operating under false names, or travelling with different security measures—that are withheld from the regular citizens. However a person feels about gun laws or financial policies, such laws specifically treat the rich and powerful differently than the rest.

"This bears repeating: The laws of the United States stipulate that if you have more money you can invest in business opportunities that people with less money cannot. The specific amounts and details are changed by Congress over time, but we are absolutely a capitalist nation where the laws give higher benefits to the rich.

"In fact, many of these laws, including all the examples above, specifically benefit the wealthy to the detriment of salary or wage earners. Regular working people are excluded by law from the best investments and various other perks and benefits. This system is called capitalism, and it is a bad system—much better than socialism or communism, to be sure, but not nearly as good as free enterprise.

"With all this said, the amazing thing is that this reality is basically ignored by almost everyone, mainly because those who point it out tend to be promoting socialistic solutions rather than free enterprise.

"As a result, people are accustomed to hearing those who want bigger government attacking the rich. But almost nobody has experienced those who want more free enterprise and much smaller government pointing out that the elite class has terribly unfair legal advantages in our society—and that this is a bad system.

"In fact, this is so deeply ingrained in most people that when they hear anyone criticizing the unfair benefits enjoyed by the rich, they pretty much never believe that the speaker is making a case for smaller, limited government and less socialism. We are so conditioned, that this possibility just does not compute for most people.

"Some may say that we are overstating this point. 'Of course the rich and powerful are treated differently than the rest. After all, they are rich and powerful!' While this may be true, it is a symptom of aristocratic society with preferential class divisions. And in nations where the laws and government treat the rich and powerful differently, freedom is always in decline."[6]

Throughout history, when we have gained our freedoms back in such nations, it has almost always been led by the leaders of the six private sectors.

"In free enterprise systems, the law allows all people to take part in any investments. If there are laws about bodyguards, firearms, using false names, or anything else, they are the same for every single citizen in the nation. This is what free enterprise means, because such a system gives everyone truly equal opportunities.

"If this seems abstract, or too surprising to be true, try starting a business in your local area. In fact, start two. Let the local zoning commissions, city council and other regulating agencies know that you are starting a business, that it will employ you and two employees, and then keep track of what fees you must pay and how many hoops you must jump through. At the same time, have your agent announce to the same government officials that a separate company, a big corporation, is bringing in a large enterprise that will employ 4,000 people — all of whom will pay taxes to the local area and bring growth and prestige. (Don't really announce this — because if it's untrue you might be breaking the law, unlike big corporations that are allowed in many places to float such trial balloons routinely.)

"Then simply sit back and watch how the two businesses are treated. In most towns, counties and cities in the United States, the small business will face an amazing amount of red tape, meetings, filings and obstacles — the big business will likely be courted and given waivers, benefits and government-funded publicity. Add up the cost to government of both of your proposed businesses, and two things will likely surprise you: 1) how much you will have to spend to set up a small business, and 2) how much the government will be willing to spend to recruit the large business.

"This is the natural model in a capitalist system. Capital gets special benefits and a different level of treatment by the government. The result in such a system is that the rich get richer, the poor get poorer, entrepreneurialism is discouraged, and many jobs, innovation, investments and growth move to other nations."[7] Freedom always declines in such an environment, unless wise leaders from the six private sectors step up and change things.

"In contrast, under free enterprise, everyone is treated the same by the law. Free enterprise is a better system than capitalism — it provides more freedom, opportunity and prosperity to many more people. All of this is more than a mere philosophical or semantic argument about which words we should use. The truth is that many people, probably most people, who feel positively about capitalism actually mean free enterprise when they say 'capitalism.' The things they admire about 'capitalism' aren't special benefits to the rich, but rather a true free market where everyone is treated equally by the law and where each person has true and equal freedom of opportunity.

"The problem is that this definition of capitalism seldom makes its way into official government policies or the law. People support free enterprise, which they call 'capitalism,' and the government implements public policy that is certainly capitalism (because it favors those with more capital) but violates the principles of free enterprise. This 'bait and switch' is one of the main problems with using the term *capitalism*.

"If by capitalism we mean true economic freedom and laws that treat everyone the same, regardless of their level of wealth, and if this thing we call capitalism made it into our laws and became our operational policies, I would ardently support it.

"In fact, I would support such a system whether we called it free enterprise, capitalism, or even zebra- or giraffe-ism. The system, not the label, is the important thing.

"The problem occurs when people support a thing called capitalism because they believe it is free economics for all, and then those in power take this popular support and use it to enforce something very different. This is the current reality, and it is hurting the middle and lower classes by decreasing their opportunities and abilities to prosper. Again, most people don't even realize this is happening to them.

"In short, call it what you will, but we need a system of truly free economics with laws that treat everyone the same. Words mean things, and the word *capitalism* emphasizes capital just as naturally as the phrase *free enterprise* promotes freedom and enterprise."[8] Leaders from all six private sectors need to help the rest of the people clearly understand this reality. When they don't, they become part of the problem. When they do help people understand this situation, they are great leaders for freedom.

And only such leaders can really help the nation understand this important reality. They have the credibility and stature to stand for freedom, if they will. When leaders from any, or all, of the six private sectors do this, freedom flourishes. When such leaders take action, voluntarily and boldly standing up for freedom, nations prosper.

Enterprise: "To boldly go
where no one has gone before."

5

THE THREE ECONOMIES

*"I don't disagree with what you're saying," the
woman said. "I'm just trying to get my head
around the fact that your focus is nuance."*

She paused, but I just smiled.

*"Who does that?" she continued. "Nuance? Really?
All anyone ever focuses on today is the big theme.
The headline. The story. Yes, we talk about the details
behind the story, but it's all about the headline,
not the little, seemingly unrelated nuances."*

*"That's because you're not in business; you're in academia
and media," I said. "And your topic is politics."*

*She sat back in her seat. "You mean..." She
grasped for words. "You mean in business,
they actually emphasize nuance?"*

"Yes," I replied. "Maybe not always but certainly often. Routinely, in fact." I could see she was struggling with this idea, so I continued, "Sit around with a group of top business leaders and ask them about anything. Any topic. You'll be surprised by the nuance in their answers. In fact, you'll often find the same among top religious and journalistic leaders."

She pondered, clearly remembering various conversations. She slowly nodded and grudgingly said, "You know, you're right."

There are three economies in modern society. They all matter. But most people only know about two of them. They know the third exists, in a shadowy, behind-the-scenes way that confuses most people. But the first two economies are present, pressing, and obvious. So people just focus on these two.

Point #1: The First Two Economies

A couple of recent conversations brought these economies even more to the forefront of my thinking. First, I was meeting with an old friend, touching base about the years since we'd talked together. He mentioned that his oldest son is now in college and how excited he is for his son's future. I asked what he meant, and he told me an interesting story.

Nearly thirty years ago, he ran into another of our high school friends while he was walking into his community college administration building. The two greeted each other, and they started talking. My friend told his buddy that he was there to dis-enroll from school. "I just can't take this anymore," he told him. "College is getting me nowhere."

"Well, I disagree," his buddy said. "I'm here to change my major. I'm going to get a teaching credential and teach high school. I want a steady job with good benefits."

Fast forward almost thirty years. My friend ran into this same old buddy a few weeks ago and asked him what he was doing. "Teaching high school," he replied.

"Really? Well, you told me that was your plan. I guess you made it happen. How much are you making, if you don't mind me asking?"

When his friend looked at him strangely, he laughed and said, "I only ask because you told me you wanted a steady job with good benefits, and I wanted to get out of school and get on with real life. Well, I quit school that day, but I'm still working in a dead-end job. Sometimes I wonder what I'd be making if I had followed you into the admin building that day and changed majors with you."

After a little more coaxing, the friend noted that he didn't make much teaching, only about $40,000 a year—even with tenure and more than twenty-five years of seniority. "But it's steady work, like I had hoped. Still, I've got way too much debt."

After telling me this story, my old high school friend looked at me with what can only be described as slightly haunted eyes. "When he told me he makes $40K a year, I just wanted to scream," my friend said.

"Why?" I asked.

He could tell I didn't get what he was talking about, so he sighed and looked me right in the eyes. "I've worked forty- to sixty-hour weeks every month since I walked off that campus," he told me. "And last year, I made about $18,000 working for what amounts to less than minimum wage in a convenience store. I should have stayed in college."

Those are the two economies. One goes to college, works mostly in white-collar settings, and makes from $30,000 up to about $70,000, or more, a year. Some members of this group go on to professional training and make a bit more. The people in the other group, the second economy, mostly make less than $50,000 a year, often half or a third of this amount, and frequently wish they had made different educational choices.

The people in these two economies look at each other strangely, a bit distrustfully, wondering "what could have been" if they'd taken the other path.

That's the tale of two economies. But Mark Twain may have been hinting about the third economy when he wrote in *Following the Equator*:

> *She was not quite what you would call refined.*
> *She was not quite what you would call unrefined.*
> *She was the kind of person that keeps a parrot.*

What does this mean, exactly? Simply that most people understand the first two economies, but the third economy is elusive for most people. They don't quite grasp it. In fact, you may be wondering what I'm talking about right now.

Point # 2: The Third Economy

This brings me to our main point in this chapter. Ask members of the first two economies for advice about education and work, and they'll mostly say the same thing. "Get good grades, go to college, and get a good career. Use your educational years to set yourself up for a steady job with good benefits." This is the advice my grandfather gave my father at age twenty and the same counsel my dad gave me after high school. Millions of fathers and mothers have supplied the same recommendations over the past fifty years.

This advice makes sense if all you know are the two economies. Sadly, the third economy is seldom mentioned. It is, in fact, patently ignored in most families. Or it is quickly discounted if anyone is bold enough to bring it up.

A second experience illustrates this reality. I recently visited a doctor for a scheduled appointment. During the small talk, he mentioned that his younger grandchildren are in college but scoffed that it was probably a total waste of time. "All their older siblings and cousins are college graduates," he said, "and none of them have jobs. They've all had to move back home with their parents."

He laughed, but he seemed more frustrated than amused. "It's the current economy," he continued. "This presidential administration has been a disaster, and it doesn't look like anyone is going to change things anytime soon. I don't know what these kids are supposed to do. They have good degrees—law, accounting, engineering—but they can't find jobs. Washington has really screwed us up."

I brought up the third economy, though I didn't call it that. What I actually said was: "There are lots of opportunities in entrepreneurship and building a business right now." He looked at me like I was crazy—like maybe I had three heads or something. He shook his head skeptically.

"Entrepreneurship is hard work," I started to say, "but the rewards of success are high and—"

"No," he said, cutting me off—not rudely but as if he hadn't really heard me. That happens a lot when you bring up the third economy. He assured me, "College is the best bet. There's really no other way."

I wasn't in the mood to debate with him, so I let it go. But he cocked his head to one side in thought and said slowly, "Although…" Then he shook his head like he was discounting some thought and had decided not to finish his sentence.

"What?" I asked. "You looked like you wanted to say something."

"Well…" He paused…and then sighed. I kept looking at him, waiting, so he said, "The truth is that one of my grandsons didn't go to college." He said it with embarrassment. "Actually, he started school but then dropped out in his second year. We were all really worried about him."

He paused again and looked at me a bit strangely. I could tell he wanted to say more but wasn't quite sure how to go about it.

"What happened?" I prompted.

"To tell you the truth, I'm not really sure. He started a business—you know, one of those sales programs where you build a big group, and they buy from you month after month. Anyway, he's really doing well. He paid off his big house a few years ago—no more mortgage or anything. He has nice cars, all paid for. And they travel a lot, just for fun. They fly chartered, real fancy. He and his wife took us and his parents to Hawaii for a week. He didn't even blink at the expense."

"That's great," I told him. "At least some people are doing well in this economy."

He looked at me with that strange expression again. "I'm not sure what to make of it," he said. "I keep wondering if he's going to finish college."

I was surprised by this turn of thought, so I asked, "So he can get a great education, you mean? Read the classics? Broaden his thinking?"

He repeated the three heads look. "No. He reads all the time, way more than anyone else in the family. He doesn't need college for that. I want him to go back to college so he can get a real job."

I laughed out loud, a deep belly laugh, it was so funny. I didn't mean to, and I immediately worried that I would offend him. But he grinned. Then he shook his head. "I know it's crazy, but I just keep worrying about him, even though he's the only one in the family who is really doing well. The others are struggling, all moved back in with their parents—spouses and little kids in tow. But they have college degrees, so I keep thinking they'll be fine. But they're not. They're drowning in student debt and a bunch of other debts. It just makes no sense."

He sighed and talked bad about Washington again. Finally he said, "I've poured so much money into helping those kids go to college, and now the only one who has any money to raise his family is the one who dropped out. It just doesn't make any sense." He kept shaking his head, brow deeply furrowed.

I left his office thinking that he was so steeped in the two economies that he didn't really believe the third economy existed. He just didn't buy it, even when all the evidence was right there in front of him.

He's not alone. The whole nation and most of today's industrialized nations, in fact, are right there with him. So many people believe in the two economies (high school/blue-collar jobs on the one hand and college/white-collar careers on the other) that most just never quite accept that the entrepreneurial economy is real.

It's too bad because that's where nearly all the current top career and financial opportunities are found. The future is in the third economy, for those who realize it and get to work. If you've got kids, I hope you can see the third economy—for their sake—because it's real, and it's here to stay. The first two economies are in major decline, whatever the so-called experts claim. Alvin Toffler warned us in his bestseller *Future Shock* that this was going to happen, and so did Peter Drucker, back when he first predicted the Information Age. Now it's happening.

I hope more of us realize the truth before it's too late. China gets it. So does India, along with a bunch of other nations. We need the six private sector leaders in our nation to realize that this is happening. The longer we take to get real and start leading in the entrepreneurial/innovative third economy (the *real* economy, actually), the harder it will be for our kids and grandkids. The third economy will dominate the twenty-first century. It already is, in fact, whether you've chosen to see it yet or not.

Truth is truth, even when our false traditions and outdated background refuse to let us see clearly.

Point #3: The Truth about Education and the Three Economies

But how does education, especially higher education, fit into the three economies? This is where it gets really interesting. A while back, I wrote an article about how too many colleges and universities aren't really preparing people well for leadership in society, and a number of people pointed out that for the most part, students (and their parents) today see college as job preparation—pure and simple.

For many people, college is now mostly about "Hire Education," as some university billboards pronounce, not Higher Education. My first response to this is: "How sad." Education once meant greatness; now it's just about getting a job.

Don't get me wrong; getting a job can be a worthy endeavor. But education can be so much more. And let's be honest; when American education was focused on greatness instead of job training, the employment rate was higher, and the overall quality and duration of jobs were better. Plus there were more successful entrepreneurs in all six private sectors.

Maybe those who embraced the old style of education for real learning, not just job training, knew something we've forgotten today. The American standard of living has decreased drastically in the last five decades, starting precisely at the same time that education reframed from greatness to job training. And this has happened around the industrialized world, not just in the United States.

By the way, our standard of living only looks similar to the 1950s because now both parents are working to pay for what one income used to cover. And even with this, most families still have to supplement their two incomes with additional debt.

But I looked even deeper into education and career statistics, just to see whether the old promise that a college degree doubles or triples your income potential is true. Guess what? There are some big myths perpetrated in the statistics on the relationship between college degrees and career earnings. The main argument that frequently gets tossed around is that those with a college degree earn much more than those without one.

It turns out this is half true and half false. If you look at some of the most popular college majors and what people do with them after graduation and compare these to many of the most popular jobs for people without a degree, it turns out that, on average, those with a four-year degree make about one-third more.

For example, sociology graduates earn an average of $47,121 a year, education grads average $52,241, religious studies grads average $61,811, hospitality/tourism $55,476, nutrition $53,679, psychology $43,384, fine arts $37,819, journalism/reporter $37,393, and communications $52,549.[9]

Many popular jobs in high-growth sectors that don't require a college degree pay less on average, including home care aide $26,266, receptionist $30,025, carpenter $44,778, office clerk $31,476, bookkeeper $39,022, meeting/event assistant $44,189, and software developer $57,916.[10]

This is what people typically mean when they say that a college degree doubles or triples a person's earning potential. Actually, it doesn't double or triple it, but on average, it boosts it by about 30 percent. That's a significant boost in earnings, for sure.

But what is left out of this statistic, what most people don't realize, is that there are two fields that do triple or quadruple a person's earning potential. In fact, these fields allow for much more than triple earnings.

The first is sales, and the second is entrepreneurship or building a business (in all six sectors). These are the third economy, and this is important news.

The numbers are interesting. For example, the average salary for a sales representative is $75,666,[11] and for an entrepreneur in a sales field, it is $165,000.[12] Neither of these requires college, though a degree may help a person get the job. Median pay for a sales executive is $127,000, and for a sales director, it is $142,000. But business entrepreneurship beats even sales.

The only major field where the average beats business entrepreneurship is medicine, where nonsurgical physicians average $199,000–$205,000 per year, and surgeons average $192,000–$299,000 annually.[13]

Even this statistic is skewed, however, because surgeons spend on average eleven years more in school than most business entrepreneurs and also start work with an average of $140,000 in student loans. Factoring in the cost of paying back the principal and interest on this debt and the eleven years of additional work, entrepreneurial earnings are on par with or higher than those of medical professionals.

Additionally, when stock, dividends, and nonsalary profits are included, doctor compensation falls far short of successful entrepreneurial careers.

Why aren't these things frequently shared with young people making education and career decisions? One reason is that most studies and statistics emphasize salaries only, not overall pay.

For example, the median starting salary for attorneys is $80,000 a year; at the height of their earning, the average is $155,000–$170,000.[14] Overall, the median salary for attorneys is $118,000.[15]

But those who make partner in top firms or build their own practices become entrepreneurs who get paid nonsalaried profits out of the firms' earnings. This ownership compensation in large firms is as much as four to eight times their annual salary. In short, business ownership frequently pays much more than a job.

Likewise, accountants generally make between $45,000 and $87,000,[16] while partners in big firms are often compensated in ownership/entrepreneurial payments of more than $400,000 per annum. Engineers make on average between $60,000 and

$120,000 per year,[17] while those who own engineering firms often make much, much more. A carpenter earns on average just under $45,000, while an owner of a contracting business can make many times this amount.

Successful franchise owners and successful network marketers make a lot more on average than those in nonentrepreneurial careers.

The view that college drastically increases earning potential persists, however. As one report put it: "Numerous studies over the years have shown that individuals with college degrees significantly outearn those with high school degrees by $1 million or more over the course of a lifetime."[18] A master's degree boosts earnings over high school by an average of $1.2 million, and a professional degree by an average of $1.7 million.[19]

While these statistics are compelling, what is left out of most articles on this topic is actually much bigger news. The third economy is real. Successful sales entrepreneurship increases earnings over high school by a lifetime average of $5.4 million[20] (or $7.4 million when bonuses, dividends, options, and other nonsalary income is included).[21]

Why isn't this the real news? The difference is huge. It's great that a college degree can bring on average an extra million dollars of earnings in life or that a law or medical degree can significantly increase this amount, but it's downright fantastic that successful business ownership can bring $5.4–$7.4 million of additional lifetime income. Again, this is the real story.

This is downplayed by many professionals who find that leaving corporate pay to start their own companies reduces their immediate income, but the true test is how much they'd have made if they had started their own company in the beginning and built it over the years. Those who successfully follow this path typically make a lot more.

Some people argue that it's not fair to count only successful business entrepreneurs, since many who start businesses fail. But the other statistics (of people with college and graduate degrees making more than high school graduates) also count only those who succeed — not the many (well over 50 percent) who dropped out or failed along the way.

The statistics and data show that business ownership is the most realistic road to high-level financial success. The truth about the connection between college degrees and career earnings, while true, simply isn't the most important news.

For years, I have promoted getting a great education because I consider it an incredibly high priority. If college is the place you want to get that education, then go for it. Find excellent mentors, hit the books, study, and learn. I think every person should pursue a quality education, whether in college or elsewhere. I've written several books about the vital importance of getting a great education, including the book *A Thomas Jefferson Education.*

In short, I'm a huge fan of quality learning and great education. I love all learning, including higher learning. Really learning is a crucially important lifetime pursuit, and reading great books, listening to great audios, and working with great mentors are all part of that.

But if the point of college is earning potential rather than getting a great education, let's get our facts straight.

The truth is clear: **Those who build a business into a successful venture typically earn a lot more on average than those who pursue most other career paths.** Many who try this path don't succeed, but that is true in all the other career fields as well. In the end, over 80 percent of America's millionaires are self-made,[22] and two-thirds of America's millionaires are self-employed entrepreneurs building a business.[23] The reality is the reality. And one of the great things about a free society like America is that becoming a millionaire, or whatever else you deem true success in your life mission (and it might be something very different in one of the other six sectors), is a real possibility. But we all need to understand the truth of how people get there.

However you get a great education (and I think everyone should!), if you want a career that can drastically increase your income and earning potential, building a business is it. Nothing else even comes close. And there are important businesses to be built in at least four of the seven sectors—education, media/ arts, business, and community. The third economy is real, and it's time we started talking more about it.

Why? Because as I said above, China, India, and Brazil, among other nations, understand that the third economy is the future of success and prosperity. If we don't realize this very soon and get to work, America will literally be left behind in the Information Economy. In fact, this is already happening. Only leadership, entrepreneurship, and innovation in all six private sectors can get us back on track.

"…the adventurous spirit, which characterizes the commercial character of America, has already excited uneasy sensations in several of the [great] powers of Europe."
— FEDERALIST 11

6

Entrepreneurship in the Snow: Uphill Both Ways!

"You're kidding, right?"

"No. Why would I?"

"I don't know. I just…" He sat back and sighed. "You really think business leaders have solutions? They're so focused on…profit. On making money, or getting promoted. I read LeaderShift *by you and Orrin Woodward, and my first thought was 'If only business leaders were really like this!'"*

"You think politicians are different?"

"Yes! Very. We've learned to study the details. To know the history of what happened, of what's already been tried. My first year in office, I tried to get by on theory and ideas, but it just didn't fly. I had to learn the history of every resolution and bill on the topic that's ever been

tried — here and at other levels of government as well — and all the court cases and past media reports on the issue."

"Where did you learn to do that?"

"I learned it here, in this office."

"But where did you learn the skills that made you able to read the reports and really know what to look for and actually see it when you read it?"

He looked at me and then smiled. "I see where you're headed. Well, you're right. I learned it running my business."

"And has what you learned here made you better at your business?"

He thought about that. "No. Not much, if at all."

"But when you spend long periods at home on your business, are you better at this job when you return?"

"Always." He grinned. "I get your point."

Leaders and entrepreneurs provide another essential benefit to society: They do really hard things that nobody else wants to do. I write a lot about entrepreneurship because it is vital to a free society. Without it, there is no "enterprise" in free enterprise.

Four Questions

In response to an article I wrote about the vital importance of entrepreneurship to liberty, a friend contacted me with several very good questions. These included:

1. If someone would love to start his or her own business but grew up poor and doesn't have enough capital for a startup, what can he or she do? It's not the government's proper role to loan money, so that won't help. How can entrepreneurship flourish if it's almost impossible for most people?

2. Given question #1, isn't entrepreneurship dependent on affluence, meaning that the rich just get richer because only wealthy people have the capital to help their young people entrepreneur?

3. If a person doesn't come from an affluent family and nobody teaches him or her the process, how can that person possibly succeed as an entrepreneur?

4. We know entrepreneurship is important, but it seems pretty utopian to think that regular people can do it. Is there a *realistic* way to overcome this?

Excellent questions. To answer, let's start with the big cultural problem with entrepreneurship. Most families don't teach their kids how to entrepreneur or have the capital to help them get started.

Moreover, most lower- and middle-class families actually teach their kids to avoid entrepreneurship. "It's too hard." "Too many people who try, fail." "Get a good, secure job with good benefits; that's the best path." "Only a few can entrepreneur — and you're not one of the few."

The Forgotten Fight

In such a culture, the obvious path to entrepreneurship (in all six private sectors) is lost. What is it? Most people don't even know. Historically, if my parents weren't entrepreneurs but made their living as employees, I likely wouldn't have the capital or the know-how to easily entrepreneur. In fact, I'd likely deal with some resistance from my parents, siblings, aunts and uncles, and grandparents who would wonder why I was fighting the system — or worse, why I was wasting my life.

Actually, almost every successful entrepreneur I know has followed this exact pattern. They had to figure it out on their own, and they had to deal with family concerns and some opposition. In other words, entrepreneurial success isn't part of a utopia. *It's what some people choose to do no matter how bad the system is, no matter how difficult it is to succeed.*

Let's be clear. There are a lot of successful entrepreneurs in all six private sectors today — a lot of them. There are many thousands of self-made millionaires whose parents gave them no direct financial help at all, who started with a couple hundred dollars — and in some cases, with less than ten bucks in their pocket — and built real prosperity. That's how entrepreneurship works.

There is an excellent book on this topic, *The Millionaire Next Door*, by Thomas J. Stanley and William D. Danko. The authors researched millionaires in the United States and found that 80 percent of them are self-made, meaning that they came from lower- or middle-class families and had to scratch and claw, work and fail, and keep trying in order to succeed. Their parents didn't give them capital or know-how, but these people did it anyway. Only 20 percent of millionaires came from wealthy parents or backgrounds and had help — financial, informational, etc. The 80 percent initiated it mostly themselves.

Moreover, as noted above, Stanley and Danko found that two-thirds of America's millionaires are self-employed entrepreneurs building a business (while a third either inherited wealth or earned it in jobs). This is big! Two-thirds are entrepreneurs, and the large majority of them are self-made.

For those who don't think anyone can start a business today and compete in our increasingly regulated and class-divided society, many thousands of new business owners are proving that it can still be done.

In addition, there are many entrepreneurs in the community, education, media, family, and charitable sectors who don't focus on making money but instead on directly blessing the lives of people in our society. Of course, business entrepreneurs bless a lot of lives too, and at times even more deeply, by providing jobs. But for those who want to create nonprofit or mainly service organizations, social entrepreneurship is still the most effective means of making a real difference.

All entrepreneurship — both for-profit and not-for-profit — is challenging, but a lot of people are making their business or social enterprises thrive.

It's hard, yes. It's harder than it was fifty or thirty or even seven years ago, yes. Many fail. But it is still possible. Not utopian. Not easy. Very difficult. But possible — and deeply needed.

Sadly, the incredible expansion of government regulations has made starting any business increasingly difficult. Government policy favors big entities with a lot of capital. It's harder on the little guy, the startup. Still, twenty years from now, there will be thousands of additional people who are millionaires or at least very successful financially who today can barely pay their bills. And there will be those in nonprofit roles continuing to provide amazing social programs that help many people without taking a dime from the government because they run on private enterprise.

The Reality Is Surprising

The large majority of them will be entrepreneurs. And they will entrepreneur in ways that serve and lead all of the six private sectors in our society. Regardless of their background, government policies, trends, and increasing class divides, thousands will simply keep at it until they succeed.

Again, it's no utopia. Most will do it against the advice of certain family members and friends. (That's a truly sad commentary on our society.) And they'll do it in spite of no help or even opposition from loved ones. Most will do it without adequate capital—or hardly any capital—at first. Most will fail at times along the way and keep trying until they succeed.

Most will be surprised by just how hard it is. When they do finally succeed, most will find that other people consider them lucky, though such people could have the same results if they would make the same choices and do the same hard things.

An Entrepreneurial Society?

So how can we create a society that really, truly encourages entrepreneurial leadership in all six sectors? First, some people are just going to do it regardless of what the obstacles are. That's the only way, ultimately.

Second, we need a society that values entrepreneurship in all six private sectors enough that government will change its enterprise-killing policies and regulations. Just look at the states where governors make this a priority—even when Congress or the White House enacts more anti-small business policies—and the states with governors who don't. The results are drastically different.

And third, each of us can do a lot more as leaders in our homes and careers. We all need to promote business and social entrepreneurship. Parents, teachers, friends, scholars, journalists, writers, artists, actors, producers, clergy, investors, politicians, and everyone else—we need to make it a real priority.

But in the meantime, the real battle is won by those who just decide to do the work of successful business ownership and leadership no matter what, who choose to "cowboy up" and work until they succeed regardless of the obstacles.

That's the opposite of utopia. *Those who do it and do it well—and those who help them do it—are heroes. I repeat: They are heroes! Pure and simple. We need a lot more of them.*

When people told Thomas Paine that the idea of fighting the British, the greatest power in the world at the time, and winning was ridiculous, he responded that it was actually just incredibly hard. *Heaven knows how to put a proper price on its goods*, he assured everyone, and it would be very surprising if something as valuable as freedom wasn't nearly impossibly hard to obtain. The same is true of successful leadership, innovation, and business and social entrepreneurship. If it were easy, everyone would do it.

It's hard, and the government seems bent on making it harder every month. Those who do it anyway, who stand up and build businesses even when it is this difficult, are today's pilgrims, today's pioneers, today's explorers, today's founding fathers and mothers. They are the true leaders of this generation. They are the heroes of all seven sectors.

We need you to become one of them. Your children need this from you. Your grandchildren need this from you. All of us need you to do this. This is what brings freedom and makes it last. All throughout history, this kind of leadership from regular citizens has been the only thing that has really caused freedom.

But my friend is right. Most people just aren't going to do this. To those who do, who face down all the obstacles and just do it anyway, our whole generation owes you a great big "Thank you!" The future of all seven kinds of leadership, especially in the six private sectors, will determine the future of freedom, for all of us.

So yes, building a business may feel like walking uphill in the snow twice a day. But honestly, this is why those who do this successfully are often such good leaders in a free society. They learn lessons of success, leadership, and influence that few people ever obtain. If you want your society to be more free, it needs more successful business owners in all seven sectors.

"The prosperity of commerce is now perceived and acknowledged by all enlightened statesmen to be the most useful as well as the most productive source of national wealth..."
— *FEDERALIST* 12

7

SEVEN KINDS OF GOVERNMENT

(We Have the Sixth Type Today, and Only the
Private Sector Is Likely to Fix This)

*"Having served as a Senator, you've gained experience
in both the business and government world. If you had to
choose one or the other," I pressed, "which career would
you do for the rest of your life? Politics or business?"*

"Business, of course," he said immediately.

"Why?" I asked.

*His grin broadened, and he said, "It's so much more
fun! And you can actually get something done."*

Every government seeks to increase its power. And power
is control over obedience, according to Bertrand de Jouvenel.
"Force alone can establish power, habit alone can keep it in
being..."

But one more thing is needed to have absolute power: credit. This means that any government wanting great power must come up with some way to openly reward people who obey its commands.

In short, any entity trying to control obedience must find a way to use force, to maintain a habit of obedience among the people, and to give credit and recognition to the most obedient. This makes obedience popular and lucrative and disobedience dangerous and unpopular.

To gain the obedience of the masses, Jouvenel taught, a government must first convince the people that they *should* obey. Whom should they obey? The government. Then it must show them that they will suffer if they don't obey but be rewarded if they do.

Wow. That's dark.

Six Bad Types and One Good Type of Government

There are seven main ways to persuade the people that they really should follow a government, and six of them have been used multiple times in history to increase the power and force of bad governments. Freedom is decreased any time the people believe any of these six:

1. The Divine Right of Kings ("God made me your ruler, and your eternal salvation depends on obeying me and my agents.")

2. Majority Rules ("If most of the people vote for it, the rest should follow, even if the vote is evil or ridiculous, because we are all part of the whole and must follow the majority decision.")

3. Benefits to the People ("If you vote for me, I'll make sure you get more of x and less of y.")

4. The Need for Order and Security ("If the government doesn't have the power to protect you, bad people will hurt you, so give us more power. We promise we'll never, ever abuse it. Just trust us.")

5. The Pure Force Doctrine ("If you don't obey us, here is what we'll do to your parents, spouse, children, reputation, body, and possessions...")

6. The Invisible Government — or a combined Pure Force and Order and Security system on steroids ("A few of us will know the secrets and make the decisions so that the rest of you can relax and enjoy life. Trust us because though historical governments have abused power, we never will. We promise.")

Any government or politician arguing any of these six dangerous doctrines should immediately set off a warning bell to every citizen. None have ever maintained their trust; all have abused their power and their people. Moreover, all six of these arguments are fallacies; not one offers a valid reason for giving power or obedience to a government.

The solution to all of these is the seventh form of government: *the Informed Citizenry*. This is the doctrine of regular citizens having 1) the vote to determine who will lead them and who will not lead them and 2) the wisdom to maintain a close watch on everything government does and to keep it in line as needed.

Without the second part of this—regular people closely monitoring government and keeping it checked—all governments end up adopting one of the six bad types. In all six, freedom is eventually lost. In fact, all six types eventually turn into the Pure Force style of government. There is no exception to this in history.

By the way, the worst type of government system is the Invisible Government. In this model, the government operates largely in secret, exerting Pure Force whenever and however it wants without effective media or citizen oversight. In fact, many people living in an Invisible Government system don't even realize that Pure Force is happening every day.

The only way to stop the six bad kinds of government is to implement the Informed Citizenry society. Without this, no free nation can last.

The American founding generation and the American framers established an Informed Citizenry model. It wasn't perfect, and because of slavery, it never fully flourished until after the Civil War. Once slavery was abolished, the Informed Citizenry system began to deepen and expand. By 1945, the United States, with less than 6 percent of the world's population, was producing over half of the globe's goods and services. Freedom works.

But freedom only lasts when the Informed Citizenry stays strong and active. Are you such a citizen?

How to Know Which System Your Government Is Following

Today we live under an Invisible Government model (with Pure Force steadily increasing in power) where a few power elites are expected to know the secrets and make the big decisions so the rest of us can just live our lives. It's as if the goal for many people today is to have a government that allows us to entirely avoid the struggles of governing ourselves.

If this trend continues, the entire freedom system of the United States (and a number of other "free" nations) will experience further decline. Determining which system your government uses is simple. How does your government and nation treat the weakest, most vulnerable, least powerful among you, *les misérables,* and how does it treat its enemies?

By these measures, Rome was powerful, but it wasn't great. Slaves, women, and children were chattel, literally owned by their masters. Enemy cities were leveled and the inhabitants tortured and killed or sold into slavery. The ground was salted so nothing could ever grow again. (As Jouvenel said, expansionism is part of the character of a nation seeking more power.)

Likewise, the British Empire of history was powerful but cruel. The lower classes were frequently treated like slaves (read Dickens, for example), the wealthy were allowed to be smug and domineering, and the people in foreign colonies such as India and Africa were consistently mistreated. Money and power were used to manipulate nearly every transaction and relationship.

In contrast, once slavery was abolished in the United States, America stood for the principle of freedom to millions around the world. It had raised a Statue of Liberty in the New York Harbor and invited all the poor and mistreated from around the world to immigrate to its shores and join it in freedom. It fought for European and Asian freedom and asked for no colonies or tributes in return.

During this era, America was at least genuinely trying to live up to the ideals of an Informed Citizenry system.

This focus has changed in recent times. How does our nation now treat the poor or struggling immigrant yearning to be free? The unborn baby? The captured enemy? We exclude, we terminate, and we torture. Yet because the regular citizen does not hold the torturer's knife, we are able to (falsely) claim a semblance of morality.

This is precisely how Invisible Government works. But when our government agents torture in the name of our protection and freedom, they act in *our* name. This means we bear responsibility — unless we attempt to decry and end such behaviors.

When they came for the unborn babies, we turned a tearful eye. But it kept happening — to millions.

When they came for the captured enemy, we turned a blind eye to torture. We played Javert, thinking the government knew best. But even if this were true, when we allow our government to torture, it will eventually turn such measures on us, the citizens. This is a law of history.

When they came for the weary immigrant, who risked his life just to send a few dollars home to feed his child like a modern Jean Valjean, we frowned in disgust and sent him on his way. Abraham, Jesus, and the bishop in *Les Misérables* would have thrown open their arms and (personal) resources of hospitality and welcome. Few of us follow their example.

We stand at a crossroads in modern America. On the one hand, we are quickly headed toward overwhelming Invisible Government that spies on us, expands its controls over us, spreads its regulations into every detail of our lives, and every day increases its tentacles of force.

On the other, we can be Informed and Active Citizens.

These are the two choices.

Sector Leadership

Leadership is needed in all seven sectors, but four of them can be especially effective in the current situation. These four sectors and their leaders are needed to help our free nations make the right choice — to become Informed and Active Citizens.

Since government naturally supports its own increased power, one or more of the other six sectors of free society must stand up and ensure that we choose to check government. In our modern society, the ones most capable of doing this well are the business sector, the education sector, the family sector, and the media/artistic sector.

Today, sadly, the education sector is almost entirely dominated by the government, so it uses its influence to avoid checking government. Even nonpublic schools, those that aren't owned by the government, are highly regulated. This sector has lost much of its ability to check government because it is no longer independent.

Education has become, for the most part, an extension of the government sector. Still, the few schools and educational voices that do check government power by the way they teach are nearly always privately owned by businesses or churches or, in the case of homeschools, by families. You can lead by helping such schools or even by starting one yourself.

The media sector can check government but seldom does. In fact, when it does actively check government, it is usually because a certain media organization is owned by a private business firm that values such checks on power. Again, as with education, the media sector faces many regulations that the government uses to purposely keep journalists from checking the state. This sector is not as far gone as education, but it is going in the wrong direction.

You can lead by using your business, career, influence, writing, art, and other resources to make the case for freedom. This is desperately needed. If nothing else, this can be part of your online interactions. In fact, it is currently the artistic, literary, and independent journalistic portion of this sector (even more than most of the professional media) that is having the most positive influence. Anyone can take part in this by making their ideas felt online and passing on quality online and printed content to others.

Finally, families have a huge influence on how the next generation is taught and how it votes, but few use this power to check government. Most that do utilize this power are headed by parents who are independent of the system to a certain extent, whose entrepreneurial or career success allows them the time, resources, and wisdom to teach their children the importance of an enlightened and involved citizenry that keeps the government in line.

In many nonentrepreneurially-minded families, this is seldom taught. You can lead in the family sector by teaching your children and grandchildren about freedom. Your example and influence can be incredibly powerful in this sector—if you use them.

In short, nearly all entities in the education, media/artistic, and family sectors that effectively and bravely promote wise checks on the government are closely intertwined with the business sector. This means that in all practicality, these are the sectors most likely to promote freedom and real checks on the overreach of government.

The Importance of Each Sector

Of course, leaders are needed in all seven sectors to help support freedom. This is not a surprise, but it is certainly a challenge. Just consider the main role of each sector. To begin with, the primary role of the family is happiness. Its leaders, parents, do whatever is in their power to provide for, protect, and teach the principles of happiness and progress to each member of the family unit.

Historically, the great danger in family leadership has been the recurring attempt to substitute *success* for *happiness*. This seldom works and, sadly, causes much unhappiness — in families and beyond.

The principal role of education in society is learning. Thus, education leaders prioritize pursuits that cause effective learning for their pupils. The great danger in educational leadership through modern history has been to focus on *training* the masses instead of *educating* each individual young person as a potential future leader. This nearly always empowers government at the cost of weakening all the other six sectors of free society.

The role of media and artistic leaders is to spread wisdom in a nation. The great historical flaw among many media and artistic leaders has been to mistake *facts* for *wisdom*. When our experts promote training above education and facts above wisdom, freedom declines. Again, this has generally given more power to government and reduced the power of media and artistic leadership in societies.

The vital role of religious and ethical leaders is to instill an understanding of and love for goodness. When this takes hold in a society, freedom, prosperity, virtue, and progress flourish. When it is reduced or lost, these all fade — to be replaced with corruption, immorality, selfishness, force, and violence.

The great danger in religious/ethical leadership is to seek *popularity* above *principle*. This always hurts society, and it always ends the role of churches and clergy in checking the excesses of government. When many leaders in the religious sector take this path, even those who have retained their stand for principle frequently lose much of their influence.

Community leaders in a free society have the role of emphasizing heartfelt service. This naturally creates trust and synergy among neighbors, groups, and the general public in a town, city, or nation.

The great danger of community leadership is to confuse community (volunteer) with government (force). When community leaders turn their influence over to government, they lose it. They can no longer check government choices that lack wisdom because they just become an arm of government itself—subordinate to it and dependent on it.

This is what has happened to most leaders in the six sectors of our society and the main reason our freedoms and nations are in decline. The vitally important role of government leaders in free society is to protect the other six roles, and the great danger comes in thinking that government has *any* role beyond protecting the other six.

Today most of our six types of leaders are weakened, afraid to influence the public sector, and/or unsure of how to proceed. Few even know that they are meant to be a check on government—that without them, the government will continue to cause the very decline it claims to be fighting.

If a solution is to come, it will almost surely come from the six types of private-sector leaders. And business leaders are the people most likely to lead from within other sectors such as their families, communities, churches, and schools. It will be business leaders of media who are likely to rehabilitate the role of media in checking the government. It will be business leaders in movies and television who are likely to refocus entertainment on checking government and rebuilding the other six sectors.

All of this is true because it is the natural and proper role of business to enterprise—to risk, to look around, see what is needed, and take initiative, and to innovate.

If business leaders don't do this, it probably won't get done. If leaders from the six private sectors don't do this, the free world will continue to move in the direction of government controls, and more freedoms will be lost. Aristocracies will rise in the name of more "equality" and "social justice," but they will be aristocracies nonetheless.

How to Win

To win this battle, what must business and other private-sector leaders do? They must use their careers and businesses to increase quality freedom-promoting projects in all six private sectors. Some of them must build effective and successful businesses, including media/artistic, family, educational, community, leadership, and nonprofit businesses. They must do this in spite of domineering governments and out-of-control regulation. And they must do it regardless of increasingly antibusiness government policies.

Whatever comes, truly innovative leaders are the heroes of our age. If they succeed in spreading great freedom-encouraging media, art, education, family relations, moral leadership, business opportunities, charitable service, and free enterprise goods and services, freedom can rebound. If their leaders see their dual role as building successful businesses and resurrecting a true free enterprise system, and they work together in this endeavor, they will naturally become an effective check on government overreach.

Voters in such a society will choose good jobs over campaign promises. But this will occur only if leaders in the six sectors give them real options, not more political-sounding rhetoric. If more people and leaders stand openly and vocally for free enterprise, we will win this battle.

If not, we won't.

This is where the future of freedom will be determined.

Great Britain's "overbearing power is derived from the vast extent of her manufactures and of her commerce" and business, "but as other nations infuse free principles into their governments," they too will rise in prosperity and power.

—James Madison, 1821[24]

8

WHY CAREER LEADERSHIP IS VITAL FOR FREEDOM

"Who said that?"

I turned to the voice in the next seat on the plane. The young man who greeted me continued talking without waiting for my response. "Can you tweet it to me?"

I smiled and looked back at my screen. The words were large, ready for a presentation:

"I have always concurred in the general principle that the industrious pursuits of individuals ought to be left to the individuals, as most capable of choosing and managing them. And this policy is certainly most congenial with the spirit of a free people, and is particularly due to the intelligent and enterprising citizens of the United States."

"James Madison," I told him. "It's a great quote, isn't it?"

*"Yes." He apparently thought I was too slow to
tweet it, so he asked, "May I?" And with my nod,
he snapped a picture of my screen with his phone.
Then he began to closely analyze the quote.*

*I turned back to my preparation, only to be interrupted
again. "That's the problem with America today," he said.
"We don't pay attention to what made our nation great."*

*I took a closer look at him. I wasn't surprised by the
words. I'd heard them many times before, but not from a
twenty-something kid in beach shorts, a T-shirt, and Ray-
Bans. The truth is I had no idea what to make of him.*

"I agree," I finally managed.

He laughed. "I'm Kyle." He held out his hand to shake.

*That was as strange as his words, a throwback to
the shaking-hands business culture of past decades.
I wondered if I was having a James Madison
moment, like in the book* LeaderShift.

*Hours later, they announced that the plane was beginning
its descent to Detroit, and I was wearing a big smile and
feeling a budding sense of hope for the future of freedom. It
turns out Kyle was flying to a big business convention. He
was two years into building his own business and excited
about reading the American founders, the classics, and any*

*other book on freedom or "Western Civ," as he called it, and
he now had a long list of books I'd just recommended to him.*

*"All my friends are the same way," he assured me. "We
realize that the future is up to us, and, no offense, your
generation hasn't done so well. We're going to do better."
Then he said something unexpected: "I promise."*

He said it quietly, with assurance. And I believed him.

*I got the feeling that by the words "your generation" he
meant anyone older than, maybe, twenty-six or twenty-
seven. But as we deplaned and I headed for my ride, I smiled.*

*I think there are a lot of people like Kyle out there
right now — thousands of them — reading, thinking,
preparing, building businesses, serving in their careers,
and even shaking hands and talking to people on planes
about topics like James Madison and freedom.*

And you know what? Their time will come!

The real reason your career, business, and freedom are
inseparably connected is the most important point in this book.
And I've saved the best for last. To get there, let's play a little
game.

Imagine you have the job of training the youth in today's
world to become great leaders for freedom — the Washingtons,
Jeffersons, Lincolns, Churchills, Martin Luther King Jrs, and

Joans of Arc for the twenty-first century. Where would you start? What would you have them read? What histories would you share with them? Above all, what values would you want them to adopt?

Value Power

Show me what values the youth of a generation deeply believe in, and I'll show you where they'll take the nation in the decades ahead. Benjamin Franklin's abolitionist values painted slavery in the worst possible light, thankfully, and three generations of young people grew up in the Northern states deeply concerned about the great blight slavery was to their nation.

Jefferson's peers grew up deeply concerned about the way the British government overreached with the Irish, and his generation of Americans kept a close eye on every policy coming out of London. When the tea stamp arrived, they thought not about "expensive tea" but about slavery, tyranny, and rights.

The generation raised during the Great Depression on values of hard work, sacrifice, frugality, fairness, and Americanism didn't hesitate when Pearl Harbor was attacked. They flocked to the enlistment lines and signed up to go across the world and fight. Many of them lied about their ages and hid health problems in order to go and serve.

It's no surprise that today's adults, raised in the shadow of Kent State and Watergate, see scandal in every presidency and cry foul at every "outrageous" government "crisis" of the week. We give Pulitzers to those who ferret out corruption, and we watch the newscasts with the most vocal and even angry anchors.

So it's also no surprise that the rising generation of youth, steeped in video replays of airliners flying into skyscrapers one after another and in reality TV characters and up-to-the-second texting of the latest memes and events, values a better world—the sooner, the better—without all the drama and empty rhetoric.

Values Now

If you wanted to train this generation to be the best leaders for freedom since the American founding, or even better (as today's youth would no doubt demand), you'd have to focus on the right values.

So let's see. What are the values that throughout history have been most closely connected with real freedom? The answer is interesting: Find a free society—from the ancient Israelites to the Athenians, from the free European merchant caravans to the Anglo-Saxons, from the free Saracens to the golden age of the Franks or the Swiss in the free Vales period, or from the Scots at their height of freedom to the American framers—and you'll find certain shared values.

The Mighty Nineteen

These start with *initiative* and *innovation*. Free people have never been loath to take action, to lead out, to see the needs and fill them.

Next come *ingenuity* and *tenacity*. Free people value overcoming problems, not giving in to them or turning to their leaders to bail them out. They hang on in hard times and figure out how to make things better.

Add to these *frugality, hard work*, and *resiliency* and then *fierce independence* and equally *fierce individualism*.

And surprisingly, you'll find a sense of *community* and *cooperation* — as long as the cooperative energy does nothing to infringe on individualism or independence. You'll also find *charity*, as long as it is voluntary. In fact, *voluntarism* is a high priority among free people. With this, you'll see a strong *dislike of force* and *dislike of castes* or social classes that force "lower" levels of people to behave differently.

In free societies, there's a strong *democratic* element, a sense of each person having a say and the group discussing and appointing its own leaders, and also republicanism, the idea of *checks and balances* on any and all authority. Free people retain *the right to fire their leaders* as well as to appoint them or *change their powers.*[25]

Here you have an amazing set of values, which in combination have dominated every truly free society in human history that lasted for more than a few years. To recap, here are some of the top values of freedom:

- Initiative
- Innovation
- Ingenuity
- Tenacity
- Frugality
- Hard Work
- Resiliency
- Fierce Independence
- Fierce Individualism
- Voluntary Community
- Voluntary Cooperation
- Voluntary Charity
- A Strong Dislike of Force

- A Strong Dislike of Social Castes/Classes
- Volunteerism
- Democratic Choice of Leaders
- Checks and Balances on Leaders
- Democratic Power to Fire Bad Leaders
- Democratic Power to Change the Authority and Powers of Leaders

These nineteen values are not only interesting because they are shared by most free societies of history, they are also fascinating for another reason. These are precisely the same values held by successful free enterprise societies and by most successful entrepreneurs (in all six private sectors) and *intrepreneurs* (those who work as employees in all six sectors and apply the entrepreneurial mindset and values in all their work).

The Nineteen in All Seven Sectors

These values are what brings success in entrepreneurial and intrepreneurial ventures. Without them, leaders fail. To the extent that they master these touchstones, business owners and intrepreneurs flourish. This is true of leadership in all six private sectors.

This isn't true in every job, by the way. A successful accountant, teacher, nurse, or engineer doesn't need all of these traits. But if the accountant tries to build his or her own firm without these values, failure is almost assured. A nurse can get by with only a few of these—unless he or she starts a nursing company or tries to increase the quality of his or her whole department, in which case, they are essential. They are also crucial if as part of his or her career, the nurse becomes a leader in the community sector and seeks to influence the whole society for good.

In short, the values of freedom don't just overlap with the values of successful business leadership and intrepreneurship; they are identical. They are the same. And they apply to the innovative-leadership types in all seven sectors.

The Most Important People in a Nation

Thomas Jefferson said that in America's free society of his day, farmers were the most important citizens. Why? Because their natural independence, innovation, frugality, and other values were the very standards needed to make a free nation succeed. Remember that in Jefferson's day, nearly all farmers were independent business owners, family leaders, community elders, and/or local educational, church, and media leaders. He was not referring to tenant farmers like European serfs or to farm laborers working as employees.

Owners, business and social entrepreneurs, intrepreneurs, and other leaders of all six private sectors are the most important citizens to the extent that they express these nineteen values, live them deeply, and effectively teach them to the rest of us. The truth is that our modern declines in freedom and opportunity are a direct result of our increasing loss of these nineteen vital values in our society.

Rekindle these values, and we'll regain our freedoms and our national clout and strength. Lose these values any more than we already have, and we'll continue to decline.

China, India, Brazil, and other nations are increasing their power because they are adopting more of these values. If they eventually adopt all of them, they'll become the world's superpowers. The values are that powerful—and that certain.

Your Real Career

To put America squarely on the right path, we must educate our people in these nineteen free-enterprise values—the entrepreneurial values, the freedom values, the leadership values. And we must instill them in all six nongovernmental sectors as well as the seventh (government) sector. If this happens, the future of freedom is bright. If not, it isn't.

This means that your leadership is essential.

The people most qualified to do such training are those who live these nineteen values. Again, this means successful leaders—in all seven sectors of free society.

The Plan

If you are such a leader, help us. Your nation needs you. The future of freedom in the world needs you.

If you are not such a leader, become one. Memorize the list of nineteen values, and make them a part of your everyday life. Become them. Live them. Exemplify them. Master them.

Whatever your career, whatever your daily life, become a master of these nineteen values. Apply them day in and day out. They will help you lead your career, your business, your sector of influence, and they will help you lead the world toward increased freedom, opportunity, virtue, and happiness.

Whatever your job, your education, your training, your life mission and purpose, whatever your career or business, the nineteen values of freedom will make you better in your work. And as you apply them each day and master them, and help others do the same, you'll have a direct influence on the future of freedom.

Your career or business will become your citizenship, your work leadership will become your patriotism, and your daily work will be your service to freedom. In truth, they are anyway, even if this isn't a conscious choice.

In the years ahead, some people will apply these values, and others will not. Those who do apply them will be the leaders, the ones who stand for freedom and a better society for everyone. These values will make you a better leader and often more successful in your career and business. They will make you a better person and a more effective adviser, friend, parent, and community member.

In short, the future of freedom depends on how you spend your time leading your family, work, and community. In free nations, our career and business leadership is always a key part of our citizenship because those who become leaders naturally lead much more than a home, a department, or a company. They lead a nation.

Your work-related enterprises will determine the future of freedom every bit as much as all the votes you'll ever cast. More, in fact.

Isn't it time that all of us recognize this, openly celebrate it, and actively do more with it? If we aren't using our careers and work to build the nation in the right way, we aren't really doing what free people do. If this continues, we won't stay a free people for long.

Freedom is the natural result of good, regular citizens from all walks of life using their daily lives, work, and careers to become real leaders in the seven sectors of a free society — and then making their influence felt. This is how freedom is maintained. Freedom isn't up to Washington, London, Ottawa, Beijing, or any elected official.

It is up to you.

It is your job.

It is your career.

It is your business.

And ultimately, your family's future happiness depends on how well you do this vitally important work.

NOTES

1   *Online Etymology Dictionary*

2   Ibid.

3   Oliver DeMille, *Free Enterprise vs. Capitalism*

4   Ibid.

5   Ibid.

6   Ibid.

7   Ibid.

8   Ibid.

9   salary.com, 2013. Unless otherwise noted, the salary statistics in this chapter were compiled in September/October 2013.

10   salary.com

11   salary.com

12   simplyhired.com

13   MedicalNews.medrounds.org; Salary.com differs on this statistic, placing the median for surgeons at $340,000 per annum. Salary.com lists oral surgeons at a median of $250,000 per year and specialized surgeons between $348,000 and $572,000. See also CNNMoney.com, "Best Jobs in America: Median Pay."

14   thelawdictionary.org; Salary.com puts the median amount between $77,000 and $150,000.

15   CNNMoney.com

16   salary.com

17   salary.com

18   salary.com

19   dba-oracle.com, based on annual averages with required schooling factored in. The statistics from the US Census Bureau reported on about.com are $900,000 more for college graduates and $1.3 million more for people with master's degrees.

20   See the US Census Bureau report details at usgovinfo.about.com and entrepreneurial sales executive average pay of $165,000 per annum at simplyhired.com.

21   This amount may actually be higher. This rate is figured at 37%, which is actually less than half the average because salary only accounts for approximately 20% of base pay for many CEOs, while 80% is paid in other compensation; see salary.com, "Executive

Compensation." Not all entrepreneurs are CEOs, but many receive significant nonsalary pay.

22 See Thomas J. Stanley and William D. Danko, *The Millionaire Next Door.*

23 See Thomas J. Stanley and William D. Danko, *The Millionaire Next Door.* See also Robert Kiyosaki, *The CashFlow Quadrant*; Andrew McAfee, "Stop Requiring College Degrees," *Harvard Business Review Blog Network.*

24 See Madison's quote in a letter to Richard Rush, November 20, 1821, in *The Complete Madison: His Basic Writings,* edited by Saul K. Padover. The original words are: "With respect to G. Britain, her overbearing power is derived from the vast extent of her manufactures and of her commerce, which furnish her naval resources. But as other nations infuse free principles into their Governments, and extend the policy they are adopting of doing for themselves what G. Britain has been allowed to do for them, she will, like the Dutch, who once enjoyed a like ascendency on the same element, be reduced within her natural sphere…"

25 See, for example, how strongly this is worded in the first paragraph of the Declaration of Independence and reemphasized throughout the document.

ACKNOWLEDGMENTS

Every book is a cooperative symphony of many talented people. A special thank you to Emma Cox, Rachel DeMille, and Sara DeMille for countless hours of help on the manuscript. Orrin Woodward, Chris Brady, and Stephen Palmer are a constant source of ideas and inspiration.

The Obstaclés Press team is a joy to work with. Thanks to Michelle Turner, Norm Williams, Deborah Brady, and Paul Hawley for their editorial and publication expertise and to Vernie Lynn DeMille for the cover design.

ABOUT THE AUTHOR

Oliver DeMille is a *New York Times, Wall Street Journal,* and *USA Today* bestselling author and a popular keynote speaker. He is the author or coauthor of *Leadership Education, FreedomShift, The Coming Aristocracy, 1913, The Student Whisperer, LeaderShift, We Hold These Truths to Be Self-Evident,* and *The U.S. Constitution and the 196 Indispensable Principles of Freedom.* He is also the founder of the Thomas Jefferson Education (TJEd) style of learning and a founder of The Center for Social Leadership. Oliver and his wife Rachel have eight children.

Connect with Oliver at oliverdemille.com
and on Facebook, Twitter, and LinkedIn.